ACCOMPANIMENTS

FOR UNISON HYMN-SINGING

ACCOMPANIMENTS
FOR UNISON HYMN-SINGING

Compiled and Edited by

Gerald H. Knight

THE ROYAL SCHOOL OF CHURCH MUSIC
ADDINGTON PALACE, CROYDON, CR9 5AD, ENGLAND

ACKNOWLEDGEMENTS

The Royal School of Church Music is grateful for the free use of the following copyright material:

HYMNS ANCIENT AND MODERN LTD
    Laus Deo, Chislehurst
FAITH PRESS LTD
    Bow Brickhill, The Saviour of the World
SIR DAVID WILLCOCKS
    Darwall's 148th
OXFORD UNIVERSITY PRESS
    O quanta qualia

All accompaniments other than those listed above are the Copyright of the Royal School of Church Music.

First published 1981
Reprinted with amendments 1987

Reproduced and printed by
UNWIN BROTHERS LIMITED
The Gresham Press, Old Woking, Surrey
A Member of the Martins Printing Group

PREFACE

AT A TIME when considerable efforts are being made to encourage congregations to take their full share in the offering of corporate worship instead of leaving most of the singing to choirs, it seems appropriate that something should be done to re-vitalise hymn-singing. All too often the singing is lifeless and lacking in vigour, and often this is directly attributable to rhythmless and uninspiring organ accompaniment.

No directions written in a book can convert the dull or unimaginative organist into an ideal accompanist, and this book does not attempt to do that. Its objectives briefly are:—
  (i) to provide a little spice in the accompaniment of unison verses in hymns;
  (ii) to discourage those who lack the considerable harmonic and contrapuntal ability from attempting what in the hands of a master appears effortless but is in fact a fairly rare and unusual skill.

There have in the past been a number of masters of the art of free organ accompaniment, and fortunately some of them wrote down examples of their work, a few of which are included in this collection: Charles Harford Lloyd, whose *Free Accompaniment of Unison Hymn Singing* has been out of print for some years; Charles Macpherson, whose accompaniments for *Laus Deo* appeared in a book of varied accompaniments published in 1912 by the Proprietors of *Hymns Ancient and Modern*; and Sydney Nicholson, Founder of the Royal School of Church Music, to many of whose splendid accompaniments it was my privilege to sing.

Happily there are today not wanting organists possessed of this valuable skill, and they have generously allowed their accompaniments to be included in this volume. We are very grateful to them.

In offering this book for the use of organists of all kinds, it may perhaps not be out of place to add a few words of caution: first, that there are occasions when a varied accompaniment would be inadvisable, e.g. when the congregation is sparse or is unsure of itself. Secondly, the final verse of every hymn does not invariably suggest or require a varied accompaniment; judgement has to be exercised. A final cautionary word: by no means all of the accompaniments given in this book are easy to play and some of them will need to be thoroughly practised if they are to be performed with such apparent ease as to suggest that they are being improvised; an accompaniment which sounds difficult to play is always inapt.

The good accompanist of hymns is one who feels the rhythm of the tune and the moods of the words and tries to encourage the congregation and the choir to do likewise. Accuracy is not enough, nor is salvation to be found in changes of registration on the organ; both these things are necessary to good accompaniment. It is hoped that this book may encourage organists to examine their accompanying and so lead men everywhere the better to sing the praises of God.

Gerald H. Knight

ACCOMPANIMENT COMPOSERS AND TUNES

BENNETT, J. Lionel
  Dix (9)

BERTALOT, John
  Nativity (30)

BIRCH, John Anthony
  Everton (13)

BULLOCK, Sir Ernest
  Carlisle (6)

CAESAR, The Reverend Canon A. D.
  Bristol (5)

CAMPBELL, Dr Sidney S.
  Easter Song (11)

DAKERS, Dr Lionel
  Martyrdom (25)

DARKE, Dr Harold E.
  Hanover (18)

DEARNLEY, Christopher H.
  Oriel (33)

DYKES BOWER, Sir John
  Nun danket (31)

EDEN, Dr Conrad W.
  Franconia (14)

FLEMING, Michael P. M.
  Lasst uns erfreuen (20)
  Llanfair (23)

FOSTER, John
  Narenza (29)

GREENING, Richard G.
  Stuttgart (45)

GUEST, Dr George H.
  Aberystwyth (1)

HARRIS, Sir William H.
  O Quanta Qualia (32)
  Regnator Orbis (32)

HARVEY, William T.
  St Clement (39)

HOW, Martin J. R.
  Helmsley (19)

JORDAN, John W.
  St Fulbert (41)

KNIGHT, Dr Gerald H.
  Love Divine (24)
  Regent Square (37)
  St Stephen (44)

LITTLEJOHN, Charles E. S.
  Wareham (48)

LLOYD, Dr Charles Harford
    GALILEE (16)
    GERONTIUS (17)
    MELCOMBE (26)
    MOSCOW (28)
    NOTTINGHAM (43)
    PETRA (35)
    REDHEAD NO. 76 (35)
    ST ANNE (38)
    ST MAGNUS (43)

MACPHERSON, Dr Charles
    LAUS DEO (21)
    REDHEAD NO. 46 (21)

McKIE, Sir William N.
    ST ETHELWALD (40)

MASSEY, Roy C.
    WILTSHIRE (50)

NICHOLSON, Sir Sydney H.
    ADESTE FIDELES (2)
    BOW BRICKHILL (4)
    CHISLEHURST (7)
    EVENTIDE (12)
    FRENCH CAROL (15)
    PICARDY (15)
    ST JAMES (42)
    WARRINGTON (49)

PRITCHARD, Dr Arthur J.
    PADERBORN (34)

SUMSION, Dr Herbert W.
    HAST DU DENN, JESU (36)
    LOBE DEN HERREN (36)
    PRAXIS PIETATIS (36)

SURPLICE, Dr R. Alwyn
    ALL SAINTS (3)

TOWNHILL, Dr Dennis William
    LEONI (22)

VANN, Dr W. Stanley
    TRURO (46)

WAINE, Frederic
    DOMINUS REGIT ME (10)

WHITE, Peter G.
    UNIVERSITY COLLEGE (47)

WILLCOCKS, Sir David V.
    DARWALL'S 148TH (8)

WILLS, Dr Arthur W.
    MILES LANE (27)

TUNES AND ACCOMPANIMENT COMPOSERS

Tune	Composer	No.
Aberystwyth	George H. Guest	1
Adeste fideles	Sydney H. Nicholson	2
All Saints	R. Alwyn Surplice	3
Bow Brickhill	Sydney H. Nicholson	4
Bristol	Anthony D. Caesar	5
Carlisle	Ernest Bullock	6
Chislehurst	Sydney H. Nicholson	7
Darwall's 148th	David V. Willcocks	8
Dix	J. Lionel Bennett	9
Dominus regit me	Frederic Waine	10
Easter Song	Sidney S. Campbell	11
Eventide	Sydney H. Nicholson	12
Everton	John A. Birch	13
Franconia	Conrad W. Eden	14
French Carol (Picardy)	Sydney H. Nicholson	15
Galilee	Charles Harford Lloyd	16
Gerontius	Charles Harford Lloyd	17
Hanover	Harold E. Darke	18
Hast du denn, Jesu	Herbert W. Sumsion	36
Helmsley	Martin J. R. How	19
Lasst uns erfreuen	Michael P. M. Fleming	20
Laus Deo (Redhead No. 46)	Charles Macpherson	21
Leoni	Dennis W. Townhill	22
Llanfair	Michael P. M. Fleming	23
Lobe den Herren	Herbert W. Sumsion	36
Love Divine	Gerald H. Knight	24
Martyrdom	Lionel F. Dakers	25

Tune	Composer	No.
Melcombe	Charles Harford Lloyd	26
Miles Lane	Arthur W. Wills	27
Moscow	Charles Harford Lloyd	28
Narenza	John Foster	29
Nativity	John Bertalot	30
Nottingham (St Magnus)	Charles Harford Lloyd	43
Nun danket	John Dykes Bower	31
O quanta qualia	William H. Harris	32
Oriel	Christopher H. Dearnley	33
Paderborn	Arthur J. Pritchard	34
Petra (Redhead No. 76)	Charles Harford Lloyd	35
Picardy (French Carol)	Sydney H. Nicholson	15
Praxis pietatis	Herbert W. Sumsion	36
Redhead No. 46	Charles Macpherson	21
Redhead No. 76	Charles Harford Lloyd	35
Regent Square	Gerald H. Knight	37
Regnator orbis	William H. Harris	32
St Anne	Charles Harford Lloyd	38
St Clement	William T. Harvey	39
St Ethelwald	William N. McKie	40
St Fulbert	John W. Jordan	41
St James	Sydney H. Nicholson	42
St Magnus (Nottingham)	Charles Harford Lloyd	43
St Stephen	Gerald H. Knight	44
Stuttgart	Richard G. Greening	45
Truro	W. Stanley Vann	46
University College	Peter G. White	47
Wareham	Charles E. S. Littlejohn	48
Warrington	Sydney H. Nicholson	49
Wiltshire	Roy C. Massey	50

ACCOMPANIMENTS

FOR UNISON HYMN-SINGING

I. ABERYSTWYTH

Tune by Joseph Parry (1841–1903).
Accompaniment by Dr George H. Guest, Organist, St John's College, Cambridge.

2. ADESTE FIDELES

Tune from *An Essay on Church Plain Chant*, 1782.
Accompaniment by Sir Sydney H. Nicholson (1875–1947), formerly Organist, Westminster Abbey, and founder of the Royal School of Church Music.

3. ALL SAINTS

Tune from *Darmstadt Gesangbuch*, 1698.
Accompaniment by Dr R. Alwyn Surplice (1906–77) formerly Organist of Winchester Cathedral.

4. BOW BRICKHILL

Melody and accompaniment from the cantata *The Saviour of the World*, by Sir Sydney H. Nicholson (1875–1947), founder of the Royal School of Church Music.

Both settings were composed for use with the hymn 'We sing the praise of him who died'. **A** was for the verse 'It makes the coward spirit brave', and **B** for the doxology 'To Christ, who won for sinners grace'.

5. BRISTOL

Tune from Thomas Ravenscroft's *Psalms*, 1621.
Accompaniment by the Reverend Canon Anthony D. Caesar, Sub-Dean of Her Majesty's Chapels Royal.

6. CARLISLE

Tune by C. Lockhart (1745–1815).
Accompaniment by Sir Ernest Bullock (1890–1979), formerly Organist, Westminster Abbey, and one-time Chairman of the Council of the Royal School of Church Music.

7. CHISLEHURST

Tune and accompaniment by Sir Sydney H. Nicholson (1875–1947), to be sung in the chapel of the College of St Nicolas, Chislehurst, Kent, of which he was the Warden.

8. DARWALL'S 148TH

Tune by J. Darwall (1731–1789).
© David Willcocks 1971.
Accompaniment by Sir David Willcocks, formerly Director of the Royal College of Music; Organist, King's College, Cambridge, and one-time student of the SECM (now the RSCM).

9. DIX

Abridged from a chorale *Treuer Heiland* by C. Kocher (1786–1872).
Accompaniment by John Lionel Bennett (1867–1934).

Both settings were composed for use with the hymn 'As with gladness men of old'; **A** was for the verse 'Holy Jesu, every day', and **B** for 'In the heavenly country bright'.

10. DOMINUS REGIT ME

Tune by the Reverend John Bacchus Dykes (1823–1876).
Accompaniment by Frederic Waine (1911–1974), sometime Warden of Addington Palace, headquarters of the RSCM.

11. EASTER SONG

Melody from *Catholische Kirchengesänge*, Cologne 1623.
Accompaniment by Dr Sidney S. Campbell (1909-74), formerly Organist, St George's Chapel, Windsor Castle, and one-time Sub-Warden at RSCM headquarters in Canterbury and at Addington Palace, Croydon.

12. EVENTIDE

Tune by William Henry Monk (1823–1889).
Accompaniment by Sir Sydney H. Nicholson (1875–1947), composed for and used at a recording session in 1939 by the choir of the College of St Nicolas, Chislehurst.

13. EVERTON

Tune by Henry Smart (1813–1879).
Accompaniment by John Birch, Organist, The Temple Church, London.

14. FRANCONIA

Tune from *Harmonischer Liederschatz*, 1738, adapted by W. H. Harvergal (1793–1870).
Accompaniment by Dr Conrad Eden, formerly Organist, Durham Cathedral.

15. FRENCH CAROL (PICARDY)

The tune is a traditional French carol.
Accompaniment by Sir Sydney H. Nicholson (1875-1947).

16. GALILEE

Tune by Dr Philip Armes (1836–1908).
Accompaniment by Dr Charles Harford Lloyd (1849–1919), Organist, Gloucester Cathedral, and Precentor, Eton College.

17. GERONTIUS

Tune by the Reverend John Bacchus Dykes (1823–1876).
Accompaniment by Dr Charles Harford Lloyd from his book *Free Accompaniment of Unison Hymn Singing*.

18. HANOVER

Tune, possibly by Dr William Croft (1678-1727), from *Supplement to the New Version*, 1708.
Accompaniment by Dr Harold Darke (1888-1976) formerly Organist, St Michael's Church, Cornhill, in the City of London.

19. HELMSLEY

Tune adapted by Thomas Olivers (1725-1799).
Accompaniment by Martin J. R. How, Southern Commissioner of the Royal School of Church Music.

20. LASST UNS ERFREUEN

Melody from *Geistliche Kirchengesäng*, Cologne, 1623.
Accompaniment by Michael P. M. Fleming, Organist, St Alban's Church, Holborn, London, and Staff Tutor, Addington Palace.

21. LAUS DEO (REDHEAD NO. 46)

Tune by Richard Redhead (1820–1901).
Accompaniment by Dr Charles Macpherson (1870–1927), Organist, St Paul's Cathedral, London.
Both settings were composed for use with the hymn 'Bright the vision that delighted'; **A** was for the verse 'Lord, thy glory fills the heaven', and **B** for the verse 'With his seraph train before him'.

22. LEONI

The tune is a traditional Hebrew melody.
Accompaniment by Dr Dennis William Townhill, Organist, St Mary's Cathedral, Edinburgh.

23. LLANFAIR

The tune is by Robert Williams (c. 1781–1821).
Accompaniment by Michael P. M. Fleming, Organist, St Alban's Church, Holborn, London, and Staff Tutor, Addington Palace.

24. LOVE DIVINE

Tune by Sir John Stainer (1840–1901), Organist, St Paul's Cathedral, London.
Accompaniment by the Editor.

25. MARTYRDOM

Tune by Hugh Wilson (1766–1824).
Accompaniment by Dr Lionel Dakers, Director of the RSCM.

26. MELCOMBE

Tune by Samuel Webbe (1740–1816).
Accompaniment by Dr Charles Harford Lloyd (1849–1919).

27. MILES LANE

Tune by William Shrubsole (1760-1806).
Accompaniment by Dr Arthur W. Wills, Organist, Ely Cathedral, and a former student with the RSCM at Canterbury.

28. MOSCOW

Tune by Felice de Giardini (1716–1796).
Accompaniment by Dr Charles Harford Lloyd (1849–1919).

29. NARENZA

Tune by J. Leisentrit in *Catholicum Hymnologium*, 1587.
Accompaniment by John Foster, formerly Organist, Beckenham Parish Church, and Tutor at Addington Palace.

30. NATIVITY

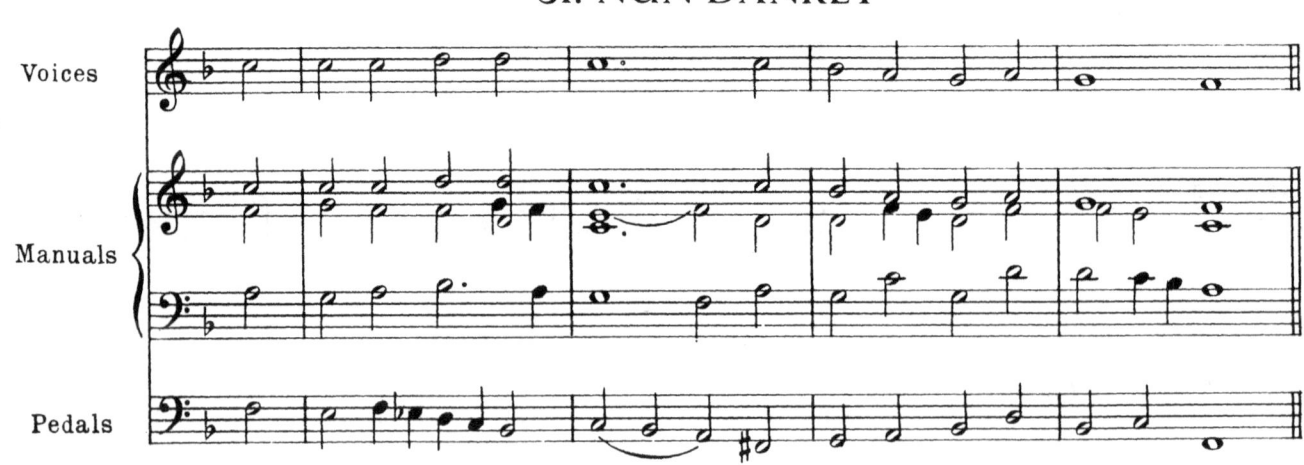

Tune by Henry Lahee (1826–1912).
Accompaniment by John Bertalot, Organist, Holy Trinity, Princeton, USA.

31. NUN DANKET

Tune by Johann Crüger (1598–1662).
Accompaniment by Sir John Dykes Bower, formerly Organist, St Paul's Cathedral, London; member of the Council of the Royal School of Church Music.

32. O QUANTA QUALIA (REGNATOR ORBIS)

The tune is adapted from a melody in La Feillée, *Méthode du plain-chant*, 1808.
Accompaniment by Sir William Harris (1883–1973), formerly Organist, St George's Chapel, Windsor Castle.

33. ORIEL

Tune by Caspar Ett (1788–1847) in *Cantica Sacra*, 1840.
Accompaniment by Christopher H. Dearnley, Organist, St Paul's Cathedral, London.

34. PADERBORN

Tune from *Paderborn Gesangbuch*, 1765.
Accompaniment by Dr Arthur J. Pritchard, formerly Organist, St John's Wood Church, London.

35. PETRA (REDHEAD NO. 76)

Tune by Richard Redhead (1820–1901).
Accompaniment by Dr Charles Harford Lloyd (1849–1919), Organist, Gloucester Cathedral, and Precentor, Eton College.
This setting was composed for the verse 'While I draw this fleeting breath' in the hymn 'Rock of ages, cleft for me'.

36. PRAXIS PIETATIS

Tune from P. Sohren's edition of *Praxis pietatis melica*, 1668.
Accompaniment by Dr Herbert W. Sumsion, formerly Organist, Gloucester Cathedral.
This setting was composed for the verse 'Praise to the Lord! O let all that is in me adore him' in the hymn 'Praise to the Lord, the Almighty, the King of creation'.

37. REGENT SQUARE

Tune by Henry Smart (1813-1879).
Accompaniment by the Editor.

38. ST ANNE

Tune, possibly by Dr William Croft (1678–1727), in *Supplement to the New Version*, 1708.
Accompaniment by Dr Charles Harford Lloyd (1849–1919).

39. ST CLEMENT

Tune by the Reverend Clement Cotterill Scholefield (1839–1904), Conduct, Eton College.
Accompaniment by William Thomas Harvey (1886–1960), formerly Assistant Organist, Canterbury Cathedral.

40. ST ETHELWALD

Tune by William Henry Monk (1823–1889).
Accompaniment by Sir William N. McKie (1901–1984), formerly Organist, Westminster Abbey, and member of the Council of the Royal School of Church Music.

41. ST FULBERT

Tune by Dr Henry John Gauntlett (1805–1876).
Accompaniment by John Jordan, formerly Organist, Chelmsford Cathedral.

42. ST JAMES

Tune by Raphael Courteville (1697).
Accompaniment by Sir Sydney H. Nicholson (1875–1947), formerly Organist, Carlisle and Manchester Cathedrals, and of Westminster Abbey.

Both settings were composed for the hymn 'Thou art the Way'; **A** was for the verse 'Thou art the Truth' and it was intended that, apart from the first four chords which were to be sung in harmony, the singing would be by sopranos (or trebles) only; **B** was for the verse 'Thou art the Life'; here, apart from the first four chords which were to be sung in harmony, the verse would be sung by men's voices only.

43. ST MAGNUS (NOTTINGHAM)

The Tune is by Jeremiah Clarke (1670-1707).
Accompaniment by Dr Charles Harford Lloyd (1849-1919).

44. ST STEPHEN

Tune by William Jones (1726–1800).
Accompaniment by the Editor.

45. STUTTGART

Tune adapted by Christian Friedrich Witt (1660-1716) from a melody is *Psalmodia Sacra*, Gotha, 1715.
Accompaniment by Richard G. Greening (1927-79), formerly Organist, Lichfield Cathedral.

46. TRURO

Tune from *Psalmodia Evangelica*, 1789.
Accompaniment by Dr W. Stanley Vann, formerly Organist, Peterborough Cathedral.
* L.H. may be played on Solo Reed from here.

47. UNIVERSITY COLLEGE

Tune by Henry John Gauntlett (1805-76).
Accompaniment by Peter G. White, Organist, Leicester Cathedral, and formerly Headquarters Choirmaster, Addington Palace.

48. WAREHAM

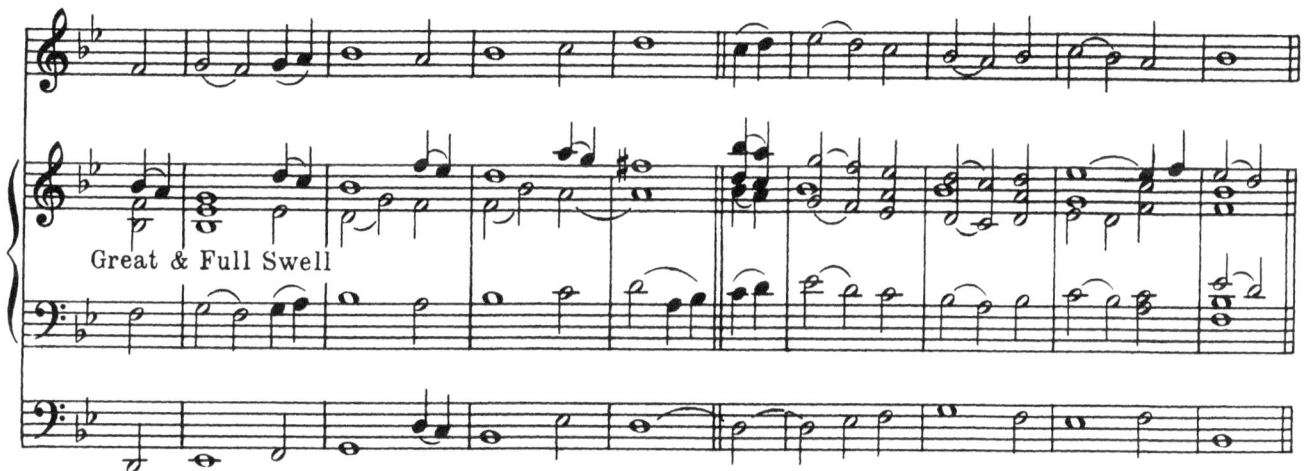

Tune by William Knapp (1698?–1768).
Accompaniment by C. E. S. Littlejohn (1879–1959), Organist, St Paul's Church, Knightsbridge, London.

49. WARRINGTON

Voices

Manuals

Pedals

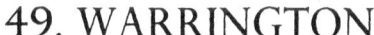

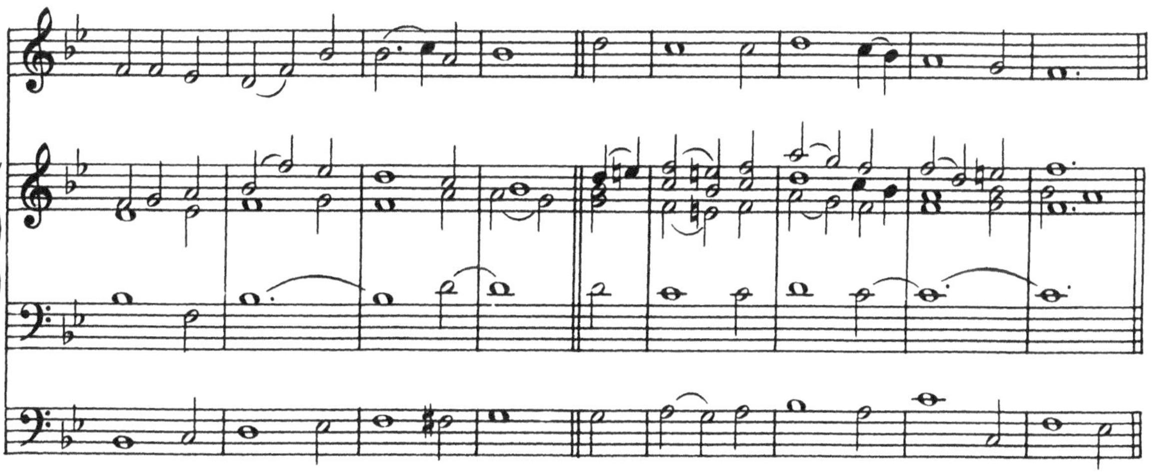

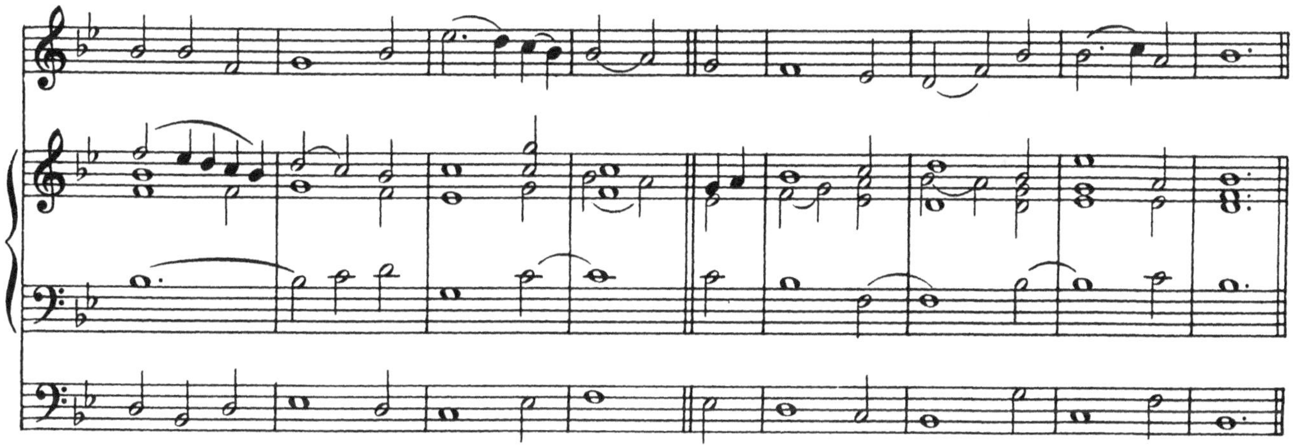

Tune by Ralph Harrison (1748–1810).
Accompaniment by Sir Sydney H. Nicholson (1875–1947).

50. WILTSHIRE

Tune by Sir George Smart (1776–1867).
Accompaniment by Roy Massey, Organist, Hereford Cathedral, formerly Warden of the Royal School of Church Music.

www.ingramcontent.com/pod-product-compliance
Lightning Source LLC
Chambersburg PA
CBHW081501040426
42446CB00016B/3348